WAGE-LABOUR AND CAPITAL

By KARL MARX

With an Introduction by
FREDERICK ENGELS

INTERNATIONAL PUBLISHERS
NEW YORK

PRINTED IN THE U. S. A.
ALLIED PRINTING TRADES COUNCIL UNION LABEL NEW YORK 65

CONTENTS

INTRODUCTION

THIS pamphlet first appeared in the form of a series of leading articles in the *Neue Rheinische Zeitung,* beginning on April 4th, 1849. The text is made up from lectures delivered by Marx before the German Workingmen's Club of Brussels in 1847. The series was never completed. The promise "to be continued," at the end of the editorial in Number 269 of the newspaper, remained unfulfilled in consequence of the precipitous events of that time: the invasion of Hungary by the Russians, and the uprisings in Dresden, Iserlohn, Elberfeld, the Palatinate, and in Baden, which led to the suppression of the paper on May 19th, 1849. And among the papers left by Marx no manuscript of any continuation of these articles has been found.

Wage-Labour and Capital has appeared as an independent publication in several editions, the last of which was issued by the Swiss Co-operative Printing Association, in Hottingen-Zurich, in 1884. Hitherto, the several editions have contained the exact wording of the original articles. But since at least ten thousand copies of the present edition are to be circulated as a propaganda tract, the question necessarily forced itself upon me, would Marx himself, under these circumstances, have approved of an unaltered literal reproduction of the original?

Marx, in the forties, had not yet completed his criticism of political economy. This was not done until toward the end of the fifties. Consequently, such of his writings as were published before the first instalment of his *Critique of Political Economy* was finished, deviate in some points from those written after 1859, and contain expressions and whole sentences which, viewed from the standpoint of his later writings, appear inexact, and even incorrect. Now, it goes without saying that in ordinary editions, intended for the public in general, this earlier standpoint, as a part of the intellectual development of the author, has its place; that the author as well as the public, has an indisputable right to an unaltered reprint of these older writings. In such a case, I would not have dreamed of changing a single word in it. But it is otherwise when the edition is destined almost exclusively for the purpose of propaganda. In such a case, Marx himself would unquestionably have brought the old work, dating from 1849, into harmony with his new point of view, and I feel sure that I am acting in his spirit when I insert in this edition the few changes and additions which are necessary in order to attain this object in all essential points.

Therefore I say to the reader at once: *this pamphlet is not as Marx wrote it in 1849, but approximately as Marx would have written it in 1891.* Moreover, so many copies of the original text are in circulation, that these will suffice until I can publish it again unaltered in a complete edition of Marx's works, to appear at some future time.

My alterations centre about one point. According to the original reading, the worker sells his *labour* for wages, which he receives from the capitalist; according to the present text, he sells his *labour-power.* And for this change, I must render an explanation: to the workers, in order that they may understand that we are not quibbling or word-juggling, but are dealing here with one of the most important points in the whole range of political economy; to the bourgeois, in order that they may convince themselves how greatly the uneducated workers, who can be easily made to grasp the most difficult economic analyses, excel our supercilious "cultured" folk, for whom such ticklish problems remain insoluble their whole life long.

Classical political economy[1] borrowed from the industrial practice the current notion of the manufacturer, that he buys and pays for the labour of his employees. This conception had been quite serviceable for the business purposes of the manufacturer, his bookkeeping and price calculation. But naïvely carried over into political economy, it there produced truly wonderful errors and confusions.

Political economy finds it an established fact that the prices of

[1] "By classical political economy I understand that economy which, since the time of W. Petty, has investigated the real relations of production in bourgeois society, in contradistinction to vulgar economy, which deals with appearances only, ruminates without ceasing on the materials long since provided by scientific economy, and there seeks plausible explanations of the most obtrusive phenomena for bourgeois daily use, but for the rest confines itself to systematising in a pedantic way, and proclaiming for everlasting truths, trite ideas held by the self-complacent bourgeoisie with regard to their own world, to them the best of all possible worlds." (Karl Marx, *Capital,* Vol. I, p. 93f.)

all commodities, among them the price of the commodity which it calls "labour," continually change; that they rise and fall in consequence of the most diverse circumstances, which often have no connection whatsoever with the production of the commodities themselves, so that prices appear to be determined, as a rule, by pure chance. As soon, therefore, as political economy stepped forth as a science, it was one of its first tasks to search for the law that hid itself behind this chance, which apparently determined the prices of commodities, and which in reality controlled this very chance. Among the prices of commodities, fluctuating and oscillating, now upward, now downward, the fixed central point was searched for around which these fluctuations and oscillations were taking place. In short, starting from the price of commodities, political economy sought for the value of commodities as the regulating law, by means of which all price fluctuations could be explained, and to which they could all be reduced in the last resort.

And so classical political economy found that the value of a commodity was determined by the labour incorporated in it and requisite to its production. With this explanation it was satisfied. And we too may for the present stop at this point. But to avoid misconceptions, I will remind the reader that to-day this explanation has become wholly inadequate. Marx was the first to investigate thoroughly into the value-forming quality of labour and to discover that not all labour which is apparently, or even really, necessary to the production of a commodity, imparts under all circumstances to this commodity a magnitude of value corresponding to the quantity of labour used up. If, therefore, we say to-day in short, with economists like Ricardo, that the value of a commodity is determined by the labour necessary to its production, we always imply the reservations and restrictions made by Marx. Thus much for our present purpose; further information can be found in Marx's *Critique of Political Economy,* which appeared in 1859, and in the first volume of *Capital.*

But as soon as the economists applied this determination of value by labour to the commodity "labour," they fell from one contradiction into another. How is the value of "labour" determined? By the necessary labour embodied in it. But how much labour is embodied in the labour of a labourer for a day, a week.

a month, a year? The labour of a day, a week, a month, a year. If labour is the measure of all values, we can express the "value of labour" only in labour. But we know absolutely nothing about the value of an hour's labour, if all that we know about it is that it is equal to one hour's labour. So thereby we have not advanced one hair's breadth nearer our goal; we are constantly turning about in a circle.

Classical economics, therefore, essayed another turn. It said: the value of a commodity is equal to its cost of production. But what is the cost of production of "labour"? In order to answer this question, the economists are forced to strain logic just a little. Instead of investigating the cost of production of labour itself, which, unfortunately, cannot be ascertained, they now investigate the cost of production of *the labourer*. And this latter can be ascertained. It changes according to time and circumstances, but for a given condition of society, in a given locality, and in a given branch of production, it, too, is given, at least within quite narrow limits. We live to-day under the regime of capitalist production, under which a large and steadily growing class of the population can live only on the condition that it works for the owners of the means of production—tools, machines, raw materials, and means of subsistence—in return for wages. On the basis of this mode of production, the labourer's cost of production consists of the sum of the means of subsistence (or their price in money) which on the average are requisite to enable him to work, to maintain in him this capacity for work, and to replace him at his departure, by reason of age, sickness, or death, with another labourer—that is to say, to propagate the working class in required numbers.

Let us assume that the money price of these means of subsistence averages 3 shillings a day. Our labourer gets therefore a daily wage of 3 shillings from his employer. For this, the capitalist lets him work, say, twelve hours a day. Our capitalist, moreover, calculates somewhat in the following fashion: Let us assume that our labourer (a machinist) has to make a part of a machine which he finishes in one day. The raw material (iron and brass in the necessary prepared form) costs 20 shillings. The consumption of coal by the steam-engine, the wear and tear of this engine itself, of the turning-lathe, and of the other tools with which our labourer works, represent for one day and one labourer a value of 1 shilling. The wages for one day are, according to our assumption, 3 shillings. This makes a total of 24 shillings for our piece of a machine.

But the capitalist calculates that on an average he will receive for it a price of 27 shillings from his customers, or 3 shillings over and above his outlay.

Whence do the 3 shillings pocketed by the capitalist come? According to the assertion of classical political economy, commodities are in the long run sold at their values, that is, they are sold at prices which correspond to the necessary quantities of labour contained in them. The average price of our part of a machine —27 shillings—would therefore equal its value, *i.e.,* equal the amount of labour embodied in it. But of these 27 shillings, 21 shillings were values already existing before the machinist began to work; 20 shillings were contained in the raw material, 1 shilling in the fuel consumed during the work and in the machines and tools used in the process and reduced in their efficiency to the value of this amount. There remains 6 shillings, which have been added to the value of the raw material. But according to the supposition of our economists themselves, these 6 shillings can arise only from the labour added to the raw material by the labourer. His twelve hours' labour has created, according to this, a new value of 6 shillings. Therefore, the value of his twelve hours' labour would be equivalent to 6 shillings. So we have at last discovered what the "value of labour" is.

"Hold on there!" cries our machinist. "Six shillings? But I have received only 3 shillings! My capitalist swears high and dry that the value of my twelve hours' labour is no more than 3 shillings, and if I were to demand six, he'd laugh at me. What kind of a story is that?"

If before this we got with our value of labour into a vicious circle, we now surely have driven straight into an insoluble contradiction. We searched for the value of labour, and we found more than we can use. For the labourer the value of the twelve hours' labour is 3 shillings; for the capitalist it is 6 shillings, of which he pays the workingman 3 shillings as wages, and pockets the remaining 3 shillings himself. According to this, labour has not one but two values, and, moreover, two very different values!

As soon as we reduce the values, now expressed in money, to

labour-time, the contradiction becomes even more absurd. By the twelve hours' labour a new value of 6 shillings is created. Therefore in six hours the new value created equals 3 shillings—the amount which the labourer receives for twelve hours' labour. For twelve hours' labour the workingman receives, as an equivalent, the product of six hours' labour. We are thus forced to one of two conclusions: either labour has two values, one of which is twice as large as the other, or twelve equals six! In both cases we get pure absurdities. Turn and twist as we may, we will not get out of this contradiction as long as we speak of the buying and selling of "labour" and of the "value of labour." And just so it happened to the political economists. The last offshoot of classical political economy—the Ricardian school—was largely wrecked on the insolubility of this contradiction. Classical political economy had run itself into a blind alley. The man who discovered the way out of this blind alley was Karl Marx.

What the economists had considered as the cost of production of "labour" was really the cost of production, not of "labour," but of the living labourer himself. And what this labourer sold to the capitalist was not his labour. "So soon as his labour really begins," says Marx, "it ceases to belong to him, and therefore can no longer be sold by him." At the most, he could sell his *future* labour, *i.e.,* assume the obligation of executing a certain piece of work in a certain time. But in this way he does not sell labour (which would first have to be performed), but for a stipulated payment he places his labour-power at the disposal of the capitalist for a certain time (in case of time-wages), or for the performance of a certain task (in case of piece-wages). He hires out or sells his *labour-power.* But this labour-power has grown up with his person and is inseparable from it. Its cost of production therefore coincides with his own cost of production; *what the economists called the cost of production of labour is really the cost of production of the labourer, and therewith of his labour-power.* And thus we can also go back from the cost of production of labour-power to the value of labour-power, and determine the quantity of social labour that is required for the production of a labour-power of a given quality, as Marx has done in the chapter on the "The Buying and Selling of Labour-Power."[1]

[1] *Capital,* Vol. I, Part II. Chapter 6.

Now what takes place after the worker has sold his labour-power, *i.e.,* after he has placed his labour-power at the disposal of the capitalist for stipulated wages—whether time-wages or piece-wages? The capitalist takes the labourer into his workshop or factory, where all the articles required for the work can be found—raw materials, auxiliary materials (coal, dyestuffs, etc.), tools and machines. Here the worker begins to work. His daily wages are, as above, 3 shillings, and it makes no difference whether he earns them as day-wages or piece-wages. We again assume that in twelve hours the worker adds by his labour a new value of 6 shillings to the value of the raw materials consumed, which new value the capitalist realises by the sale of the finished piece of work. Out of this new value he pays the worker his 3 shillings, and the remaining 3 shillings he keeps himself. If, now, the labourer creates in twelve hours a value of 6 shillings, in six hours he creates a value of 3 shillings. Consequently, after working six hours for the capitalist the labourer has returned to him the equivalent of the 3 shillings received as wages. After six hours' work both are quits, neither one owing a penny to the other.

"Hold on there!" now cries out the capitalist. "I have hired the labourer for a whole day, for twelve hours. But six hours are only half a day. So work along lively there until the other six hours are at an end—only then will we be even." And, in fact, the labourer has to submit to the conditions of the contract upon which he entered of "his own free will," and according to which he bound himself to work twelve whole hours for a product of labour which cost only six hours' labour.

Similarly with piece-wages. Let us suppose that in twelve hours our worker makes twelve commodities. Each of these costs 2 shillings in raw material and wear and tear, and is sold for 2½ shillings. On our former assumption, the capitalist gives the labourer one-fourth of a shilling for each piece, which makes a total of 3 shillings for the twelve pieces. To earn this, the worker requires twelve hours. The capitalist receives 30 shillings for the twelve pieces; deducting 24 shillings for raw material and wear and tear there remains 6 shillings, of which he pays 3 shillings in wages and pockets the remaining 3. Just as before! Here also the worker labours six hours for himself, *i.e.,* to replace his wages (half an hour in each of the twelve hours), and six hours for the capitalist.

The rock upon which the best economists were stranded as long as they started out from the value of labour, vanishes as soon as we make our starting-point the value of labour-*power*. Labour-power is, in our present-day capitalist society, a commodity like every other commodity, but yet a very peculiar commodity. It has, namely, the peculiarity of being a value-creating force, the source of value, and, moreover, when properly treated, the source of more value than it possesses itself. In the present state of production, human labour-power not only produces in a day a greater value than it itself possesses and costs; but with each new scientific discovery, with each new technical invention, there also rises the surplus of its daily production over its daily cost, while as a consequence there diminishes that part of the working day in which the labourer produces the equivalent of his day's wages, and, on the other hand, lengthens that part of the working day in which he must present labour *gratis* to the capitalist.

And this is the economic constitution of our entire modern society: the working class alone produces all values. For value is only another expression for labour, that expression, namely, by which is designated, in our capitalist society of to-day, the amount of socially necessary labour embodied in a particular commodity. But these values produced by the workers do not belong to the workers. They belong to the owners of the raw materials, machines, tools, and money, which enable them to buy the labour-power of the working class. Hence, the working class gets back only a part of the entire mass of products produced by it. And as we have just seen, the other portion, which the capitalist class retains, and which it has to share, at most, only with the landlord class, is increasing with every new discovery and invention, while the share which falls to the working class (*per capita*) rises but little and very slowly, or not at all, and under certain conditions it may even fall.

But these discoveries and inventions which supplant one another with ever-increasing speed, this productiveness of human labour which increases from day to day to unheard-of proportions, at last gives rise to a conflict, in which present capitalistic economy must go to ruin. On the one hand, immeasurable wealth and a superfluity of products with which the buyers cannot cope. On the other hand, the great mass of society proletarianised, transformed into wage-labourers, and thereby disabled from appropriating to themselves that superfluity of products. The splitting up of society into a small class, immoderately rich, and a large class of wage-labourers devoid of all property, brings it about that this society smothers in its own superfluity, while the great majority of its members are scarcely, or not at all, protected from extreme want.

This condition becomes every day more absurd and more unnecessary. It *must* be gotten rid of; it can be gotten rid of. A new social order is possible, in which the class differences of to-day will have disappeared, and in which—perhaps after a short transition period, which, though somewhat deficient in other respects, will in any case be very useful morally—there will be the means of life, of the enjoyment of life, and of the development and activity of all bodily and mental faculties, through the systematic use and further development of the enormous productive powers of society, which exists with us even now, with equal obligation upon all to work. And that the workers are growing ever more determined to achieve this new social order will be proven on both sides of the ocean on this dawning May Day, and on Sunday, May 3rd.

FREDERICK ENGELS.

London, April 30th, 1891.

WAGE-LABOUR AND CAPITAL

CHAPTER I

PRELIMINARY

FROM various quarters we have been reproached for neglecting to portray the economic conditions which form the material basis of the present struggles between classes and nations. With set purpose we have hitherto touched upon these conditions only when they forced themselves upon the surface of the political conflicts.

It was necessary, beyond everything else, to follow the development of the class struggle in the history of our own day, and to prove empirically, by the actual and daily newly created historical material, that with the subjugation of the working class, accomplished in the days of February and March, 1848, the opponents of that class—the bourgeois republicans in France, and the bourgeois and peasant classes who were fighting feudal absolutism throughout the whole continent of Europe—were simultaneously conquered; that the victory of the "moderate republic" in France sounded at the same time the fall of the nations which had responded to the February revolution with heroic wars of independence; and finally that, by the victory over the revolutionary workingmen, Europe fell back into its old double slavery, into the *English-Russian* slavery. The June conflict in Paris, the fall of Vienna, the tragi-comedy in Berlin in November, 1848, the desperate efforts of Poland, Italy, and Hungary, the starvation of Ireland into submission—these were the chief events in which the European class struggle between the bourgeoisie and the working class was summed up, and from which we proved that every revolutionary uprising, however remote from the class struggle its object might appear, must of necessity fail until the revolutionary working class shall have conquered;—that every social reform must remian a Utopia until the proletarian revolution and the feudalistic counter-revolution have been pitted against each other in a *world-wide war*. In our presentation, as in reality, Belgium and Switzerland were tragicomic caricaturish *genre* pictures in the great historic tableau;

the one the model State of the bourgeois monarchy, the other the model State of the bourgeois republic; both of them, States that flatter themselves to be just as free from the class struggle as from the European revolution.[1]

But now, after our readers have seen the class struggle of the year 1848 develop into colossal political proportions, it is time to examine more closely the economic conditions themselves upon which is founded the existence of the capitalist class and its class rule, as well as the slavery of the workers.

We shall present the subject in three great divisions:

1. The Relation of Wage-Labour to Capital, the Slavery of the Worker, the Rule of the Capitalist.
2. The Inevitable Ruin of the Middle Classes and the so-called Commons [2] under the present system.
3. The Commercial Subjugation and Exploitation of the Bourgeois classes of the various European nations by the Despot of the World Market—England.[3]

We shall seek to portray this as simply and popularly as possible, and shall not presuppose a knowledge of even the most elementary notions of political economy. We wish to be understood by the workers. And, moreover, there prevails in Germany the most remarkable ignorance and confusion of ideas in regard to the simplest economic relations, from the patented defenders of existing conditions, down to the socialist wonder-workers and the unrecognised political geniuses, in which divided Germany is even richer than in duodecimo princelings. We therefore proceed to the consideration of the first problem.

[1] It must be remembered that this was written over forty years ago. To-day, the class struggle in Switzerland, and especially in Belgium, has reached that degree of development where it compels recognition from even the most superficial observers of political and industrial life.—*Translator's Note to 1891 edition.*

[2] That is the "common" people as distinct from the "noble" and "clerical" (or "religious") people. Originating in feudal times in the rank of freeman and town-burgher the "commons" or "citizens" (burgher, burghers, citizen, citizens, or bourgeois) formed the starting-point of the "bourgeoisie."—*Ed.*

[3] As stated by Engels in the Introduction, the series of articles on "Wage-Labour and Capital" remained incomplete; the pamphlet is confined almost exclusively to a consideration of the first "great division": the relation of wage-labour to capital.—*Ed.*

CHAPTER II

WHAT ARE WAGES?

If several workmen were to be asked: "How much wages do you get?" one would reply, "I get two shillings a day from my employer"; another, "I get three shillings a day," and so on. According to the different branches of industry in which they are employed, they would mention different sums of money that they receive from their respective employers for the completion of a certain task; for example, for weaving a yard of linen, or for setting a page of type. Despite the variety of their statements, they would all agree upon one point: that wages are the amount of money which the capitalist pays for a certain period of work or for a certain amount of work.

Consequently, it appears that the capitalist *buys* their labour with money, and that for money they *sell* him their labour. But this is merely an illusion. What they actually sell to the capitalist for money is their *labour-power*. This labour-power the capitalist buys for a day, a week, a month, etc. And after he has bought it, he uses it up by letting the worker labour during the stipulated time. With the same amount of money with which the capitalist has bought their labour-power (for example, with two shillings) he could have bought a certain amount of sugar or of any other commodity. The two shillings with which he bought twenty pounds of sugar is the price of the twenty pounds of sugar. The two shillings with which he bought twelve hours' use of the labour-power, is the price of twelve hours' labour. Labour-power, then, is a commodity, no more, no less so than is the sugar. The first is measured by the clock, the other by the scales.

Their commodity, labour-power, the workers exchange for the commodity of the capitalist, for money, and, moreover, this exchange takes place at a certain ratio. So much money for so long a use of labour-power. For twelve hours' weaving, two shillings. And these two shillings, do they not represent all the other commodities which I can buy for two shillings? Therefore, actually, the worker has exchanged his commodity, labour-power, for commodities of all kinds, and, moreover, at a certain ratio. By giving him two shillings, the capitalist has given him so much meat, so much clothing, so much wood, light, etc., in exchange for his day's work. The two shillings therefore express the relation in which labour-power is exchanged for other commodities, the *exchange-value* of labour-power.

The exchange value of a commodity estimated in *money* is called its *price*. *Wages* therefore are only a special name for the price of labour-power, and are usually called the price of labour; it is the special name for the price of this peculiar commodity, which has no other repository than human flesh and blood.

Let us take any worker; for example, a weaver. The capitalist supplies him with the loom and the yarn. The weaver applies himself to work, and the yarn is turned into cloth. The capitalist takes possession of the cloth and sells it for twenty shillings, for example. Now are the wages of the weaver a share of the cloth, of the twenty shillings, of the product of his work? By no means. Long before the cloth is sold, perhaps long before it is fully woven, the weaver has received his wages. The capitalist, then, does not pay his wages out of the money which he will obtain from the cloth, but out of money already on hand. Just as little as loom and yarn are the product of the weaver to whom they are supplied by the employer, just so little are the commodities which he receives in exchange for his commodity—labour-power—his product. It is possible that the employer found no purchasers at all for the cloth. It is possible that he did not get even the amount of the wages by its sale. It is possible that he sells it very profitably in proportion to the weaver's wages. But all that does not concern the weaver. With a part of his existing wealth, of his capital, the capitalist buys the labour-power of the weaver in exactly the same manner as, with another part of his wealth, he has bought the raw material—the yarn—and the instrument of labour—the loom. After he has made these purchases, and among them belongs the labour-power necessary to the production of the cloth, *he produces only with raw materials and instruments of labour belonging to him.* For our good weaver, too, is one of the instruments of labour, and being in this respect on a par with the loom, he has no more share in the product (the cloth), or in the price of the product, than the loom itself has.

Wages, therefore, are not a share of the worker in the commodities produced by himself. Wages are that part of already existing commodities with which the capitalist buys a certain amount of productive labour-power.

Consequently, labour-power is a commodity which its possessor, the wage-worker, sells to the capitalist. Why does he sell it? It is in order to live.

But the putting of labour-power into action, *i.e.*, the work, is the active expression of the labourer's own life. And this life activity he sells to another person in order to secure the necessary means of life. His life-activity, therefore, is but a means of securing his own existence. He works that he may keep alive. He does not count the labour itself as a part of his life; it is rather a sacrifice of his life. It is a commodity that he has auctioned off to another. The product of his activity, therefore, is not the aim of his activity. What he produces for himself is not the silk that he weaves, not the gold that he draws up the mining shaft, not the palace that he builds. What he produces for himself is *wages*; and the silk, the gold, and the palace are resolved for him into a certain quantity of necessaries of life, perhaps into a cotton jacket, into copper coins, and into a basement dwelling. And the labourer who for twelve hours long, weaves, spins, bores, turns, builds, shovels, breaks stone, carries hods, and so on—is this twelve hours' weaving, spinning, boring, turning, building, shovelling, stone-breaking, regarded by him as a manifestation of life, as life? Quite the contrary. Life for him begins where this activity ceases, at the table, at the tavern seat, in bed. The twelve hours' work, on the other hand, has no meaning for him as weaving, spinning, boring, and so on, but only as earnings, which enable him to sit down at a table, to take his seat in the tavern, and to lie down in a bed. If the silk-worm's object in spinning were to prolong its existence as caterpillar, it would be a perfect example of a wage-worker.

Labour-power was not always a *commodity* (merchandise). Labour was not always wage-labour, *i.e., free labour*. The *slave* did not sell his labour-power to the slave-owner, any more than the ox sells his labour to the farmer. The slave, together with his labour-power, was sold to his owner once for all. He is a commodity that can pass from the hand of one owner to that of another. He *himself* is a commodity, but his labour-power is not *his* commodity. The *serf* sells [1] only a portion of his labour-power. It is not he who receives wages from the owner of the land; it is rather the owner of the land who receives a tribute from him. The serf belongs to the soil, and to the lord of the soil he brings its fruit. The *free labourer,* on the other hand, sells his very self, and that by fractions. He auctions off eight, ten, twelve, fifteen hours of his life, one day like the next, to the highest bidder, to the owner of raw materials, tools, and means of life, *i.e.,* to the capitalist. The labourer belongs neither to an owner nor to the soil, but eight, ten, twelve, fifteen hours of his daily life belong to whomsoever buys them. The worker leaves the capitalist, to whom he has sold himself, as often as he chooses, and the capitalist discharges him as often as he sees fit, as soon as he no longer gets any use, or not the required use, out of him. But the worker, whose only source of income is the sale of his labour-power, cannot leave *the whole class of buyers, i.e., the capitalist class,* unless he gives up his own existence. He does not belong to this or to that capitalist, but to the *capitalist class*; and it is for him to find his man, *i.e.,* to find a buyer in this capitalist class.

Before entering more closely upon the relation of capital to wage-labour, we shall present briefly the most general conditions which come into consideration in the determination of wages.

Wages, as we have seen, are the *price* of a certain commodity, labour-power. Wages, therefore, are determined by the same laws that determine the price of every other commodity. The question then is, *How is the price of a commodity determined?*

[1] "Sell" is not a very exact expression, for serfdom in its purity did not involve any relations of buying and selling between the serf and the lord of the manor, the tributes of the former to the latter consisting in *labour* and in *kind.* It is evident that Marx uses here the word "sells" in the general sense of *alienation.—Translator.*

CHAPTER III

BY WHAT IS THE PRICE OF A COMMODITY DETERMINED?

By what is the price of a commodity determined?

By the competition between buyers and sellers, by the relation of the demand to the supply, of the call to the offer. The competition by which the price of a commodity is determined is threefold.

The same commodity is offered for sale by various sellers. Whoever sells commodities of the same quality most cheaply, is sure to drive the other sellers from the field and to secure the greatest market for himself. The sellers therefore fight among themselves for the sales, for the market. Each one of them wishes to sell, and to sell as much as possible, and if possible to sell alone, to the exclusion of all other sellers. Each one sells cheaper than the other. Thus there takes place a *competition among the sellers* which *forces down* the price of the commodities offered by them.

But there is also a *competition among the buyers*; this upon its side causes the price of the proffered commodities to *rise*.

Finally, there is *competition between the buyers and the sellers*: these wish to purchase as cheaply as possible, those to sell as dearly as possible. The result of this competition between buyers and sellers will depend upon the relations between the two above-mentioned camps of competitors, *i.e.*, upon whether the competition in the army of buyers or the competition in the army of sellers is stronger. Industry leads two great armies into the field against each other, and each of these again is engaged in a battle among its own troops in its own ranks. The army among whose troops there is less fighting carries off the victory over the opposing host.

Let us suppose that there are one hundred bales of cotton in the market and at the same time purchasers for one thousand bales of cotton. In this case the demand is ten times greater than the supply. Competition among the buyers, then, will be very strong; each of them tries to get hold of one bale, if possible, of the whole one hundred bales. This example is no arbitrary supposition. In the history of commerce we have experienced periods of scarcity of cotton, when some capitalists united together and sought to buy up not one hundred bales, but the whole cotton supply of the world. In the given case, then, one buyer seeks to drive the others from the field by offering a relatively higher price for the bales of cotton. The cotton sellers, who perceive the troops of the enemy in the most violent contention among themselves, and who therefore are fully assured of the sale of their whole one hundred bales, will beware of pulling one another's hair in order to force down the price of cotton at the very moment in which their opponents race with one another to screw it up high. So, all of a sudden, peace reigns in the army of sellers. They stand opposed to the buyers like one man, fold their arms in philosophic contentment and their claims would find no limit did not the offers of even the most importunate of buyers have a very definite limit.

If, then, the supply of a commodity is less than the demand for it, competition among the sellers is very slight, or there may be none at all among them. In the same proportion in which this competition decreases, the competition among the buyers increases. Result: a more or less considerable rise in the prices of commodities.

It is well known that the opposite case, with opposite result, happens more frequently. Great excess of supply over demand; desperate competition among the sellers, and a lack of buyers; forced sales of commodities at ridiculously low prices.

But what is a rise, and what a fall of prices? What is a high, and what a low price? A grain of sand is high when examined through a microscope, and a tower is low when compared with a mountain. And if the price is determined by the relation of supply and demand, by what is the relation of supply and demand determined?

Let us turn to the first worthy citizen we meet. He will not hesitate one moment, but, like another Alexander the Great, will cut this metaphysical knot with his multiplication table. He will say to us: "If the production of the commodities which I sell has cost me one hundred pounds, and out of the sale of these goods I make one hundred and ten pounds—within the year, you understand—that's an honest, sound, reasonable profit. But if in the exchange I receive one hundred and twenty or one hundred and thirty pounds, that's a higher profit; and if I should get as much as two hundred pounds, that would be an extraordinary, an enormous profit." What is it, then, that serves this citizen as the standard of his profit? The *cost of the production* of his commodities. If in exchange for these goods he receives a quantity of other goods whose production has cost less, he has lost. If he receives in exchange for his goods a quantity of other goods whose production has cost more, he has gained. And he reckons the falling or rising of the profit according to the degree at which the exchange value of his goods stands, whether above or below his zero—the *cost of production.*

We have seen how the changing relation of supply and demand causes now a rise, now a fall of prices; now high, now low prices. If the price of a commodity rises considerably owing to a failing supply or a disproportionately growing demand, then the price of some other commodity must have fallen in proportion; for of course the price of a commodity only expresses in money the proportion in which other commodities will be given in exchange for it. If, for example, the price of a yard of silk rises from two to three shillings, the price of silver has fallen in relation to the silk, and in the same way the prices of all other commodities whose prices have remained stationary have fallen in relation to the price of silk. A larger quantity of them must be given in exchange in order to obtain the same amount of silk. Now, what will be the consequence of a rise in the price of a particular commodity? A mass of capital will be thrown into the prosperous branch of industry, and this immigration of capital into the provinces of the favoured industry will continue until it yields no more than the customary profits, or, rather until the price of its products, owing to overproduction, sinks below the cost of production.

Conversely: if the price of a commodity falls below its cost of production, then capital will be withdrawn from the production of this commodity. Except in the case of a branch of industry which has become obsolete and is therefore doomed to disappear, the production of such a commodity (that is, its supply), will, owing to this flight of capital, continue to decrease until it corresponds to the demand, and the price of the commodity rises again to the level of its cost of production; or, rather, until the supply has fallen below the demand and its price has again risen above its cost of production, *for the current price of a commodity is always either above or below its cost of production.*

We see how capital continually emigrates out of the province of one industry and immigrates into that of another. The high price produces an excessive immigration, and the low price an excessive emigration.

We could show, from another point of view, how not only the supply, but also the demand, is determined by the cost of production. But this would lead us too far away from our subject.

We have just seen how the fluctuations of supply and demand always bring the price of a commodity back to its cost of production. *The actual price of a commodity, indeed, stands always above or below the cost of production; but the rise and fall reciprocally balance each other,* so that, within a certain period of time, if the ebbs and flows of the industry are reckoned up together, the commodities will be exchanged for one another in accordance with their cost of production. Their price is thus determined by their cost of production.

The determination of price by the cost of production is not to be understood in the sense of the bourgeois economists. The economists say that the *average price* of commodities equals the cost of production: that this is the *law.* The anarchic movement, in which the rise is compensated for by a fall and the fall by a rise, they regard as an accident. We might just as well consider the fluctuations as the law, and the determination of the price by cost of production as an accident—as is, in fact, done by certain other economists. But it is precisely these fluctuations which, viewed more closely, carry the most frightful devastation in their train, and, like an earthquake, cause bourgeois society to shake to its very foundations—it is precisely these fluctuations that force the price to conform to the cost of production. In the totality of this disorderly movement is to be found its order. In the total course of this industrial anarchy, in this circular movement, competition balances, as it were, the one extravagance by the other.

We thus see that the price of a commodity is indeed determined by its cost of production, but in such wise that the periods in which the price of these commodities rises above the cost of production are balanced by the periods in which it sinks below the cost of production, and *vice versa*. Of course this does not hold good for a single given product of an industry, but only for that branch of industry. So also it does not hold good for an individual manufacturer, but only for the whole class of manufacturers.

The determination of price by cost of production is tantamount to the determination of price by the labour-time requisite to the production of a commodity, for the cost of production consists, first of raw materials and wear and tear of tools, etc., *i.e.*, of industrial products whose production has cost a certain number of work-days, which therefore represent a certain amount of labour-time, and, secondly, of direct labour, which is also measured by its duration.

CHAPTER IV

BY WHAT ARE WAGES DETERMINED?

Now, the same general laws which regulate the price of commodities in general, naturally regulate *wages,* or the *price* of labour-power. Wages will now rise, now fall, according to the relation of supply and demand, according as competition shapes itself between the buyers of labour-power, the capitalists, and sellers of labour-power, the workers. The fluctuations of wages correspond to the fluctuations in the price of commodities in general. *But within the limits of these fluctuations the price of labour-power will be determined by the cost of production, by the labour-time necessary for production of this commodity: labour-power.*

What, then, is the cost of production of labour-power?

It is the cost required for the maintenance of the labourer as a labourer, and for his education and training as a labourer.

Therefore, the shorter the time required for training up to a particular sort of work, the smaller is the cost of production of the worker, the lower is the price of his labour-power, his wages. In those branches of industry in which hardly any period of apprenticeship is necessary and the mere bodily existence of the worker is sufficient, the cost of his production is limited almost exclusively to the commodities necessary for keeping him in working condition. *The price of his work* will therefore be determined by the *price of the necessary means of subsistence.*

Here, however, there enters another consideration. The manufacturer who calculates his cost of production and, in accordance with it, the price of the product, takes into account the wear and tear of the instruments of labour. If a machine costs him, for example, one thousand shillings, and this machine is used up in ten years, he adds one hundred shillings annually to the price of the commodities, in order to be able after ten years to replace the worn-out machine with a new one. In the same manner, the cost of production of simple labour-power must include the cost of propagation, by means of which the race of workers is enabled to multiply itself, and to replace worn-out workers with new ones. The wear and tear of the worker, therefore, is calculated in the same manner as the wear and tear of the machine.

Thus, the cost of production of simple labour-power amounts to the *cost of the existence and propagation of the worker.* The price of this cost of existence and propagation constitutes wages. The wages thus determined are called the *minimum of wages.* This minimum wage, like the determination of the price of commodities in general by cost of production, does not hold good for the *single individual,* but only for the *race.* Individual workers, indeed, millions of workers, do not receive enough to be able to exist and to propagate themselves; but the wages of the whole working class adjust themselves, within the limits of their fluctuations, to this minimum.

Now that we have come to an understanding in regard to the most general laws which govern wages, as well as the price of every other commodity, we can examine our subject more particularly.

CHAPTER V

THE NATURE AND GROWTH OF CAPITAL

CAPITAL consists of raw materials, instruments of labour, and means of subsistence of all kinds, which are employed in producing new raw materials, new instruments, and new means of subsistence. All these components of capital are created by labour, products of labour, *accumulated labour*. Accumulated labour that serves as a means to new production is capital. *So say the economists.* What is a Negro slave? A man of the black race. The one explanation is worthy of the other.

A Negro is a Negro. Only under certain conditions does he become a slave. A cotton-spinning machine is a machine for spinning cotton. Only under certain conditions does it become *capital.* Torn away from these conditions, it is as little capital as gold by itself is money, or as sugar is the price of sugar.

In the process of production, human beings work not only upon nature, but also upon one another. They produce only by working together in a specified manner and reciprocally exchanging their activities. In order to produce, they enter into definite connections and relations to one another, and only within these social connections and relations does their influence upon nature operate, *i.e.,* does production take place.

These social relations between the producers, and the conditions under which they exchange their activities and share in the total act of production, will naturally vary according to the character of the means of production. With the discovery of a new instrument of warfare, the firearm, the whole internal organisation of the army was necessarily altered, the relations within which individuals compose an army and can work as an army were transformed, and the relation of different armies to one another was likewise changed.

We thus see that the *social relations within which individuals produce, the social relations of production, are altered, trans-*

formed, with the change and development of the material means of production, of the forces of production. The relations of production in their totality constitute what is called the social relations, society, and, moreover, a society at a definite stage of historic development, a society with peculiar, distinctive characteristics. *Ancient* society, *feudal* society, *bourgeois* (or capitalist) society, are such totalities of relations of production, each of which denotes a particular stage of development in the history of mankind.

Capital also is a social relation of production. It is a *bourgeois relation of production,* a relation of production of bourgeois society. The means of subsistence, the instruments of labour, the raw materials, of which capital consists—have they not been produced and accumulated under given social conditions, within definite social relations? Are they not employed for new production, under given social conditions, within definite social relations? And does not just this definite social character stamp the products which serve for new production as *capital?*

Capital consists not only of means of subsistence, instruments of labour, and raw materials, not only of material products; it consists just as much of exchange values. All products of which it consists are *commodities. Capital, consequently, is not only a sum of material products, it is a sum of commodities, of exchange values, of social magnitudes.* Capital remains the same whether we put cotton in the place of wool, rice in the place of wheat, steamships in the place of railroads, provided only that the cotton, the rice, the steamships—the body of capital—have the same exchange value, the same price, as the wool, the wheat, the railroads, in which it was previously embodied. The bodily form of capital may transform itself continually, while capital does not suffer the least alteration.

But though every capital is a sum of commodities, i.e., of exchange values, it does not follow that every sum of commodities, of exchange values, is capital.

Every sum of exchange values is an exchange value. Each particular exchange value is a sum of exchange values. For example: a house worth £1,000 is an exchange value of £1,000: a piece of paper worth one penny is a sum of exchange values of one hundred one-hundredths of a penny. Products which are exchangeable for others are *commodities*. The definite proportion in which they are exchangeable forms their *exchange value*, or, expressed in money, their price. The quantity of these products can have no effect on their character as *commodities*, as representing an *exchange value*, as having a certain *price*. Whether a tree be large or small, it remains a tree. Whether we exchange iron in pennyweights or in hundredweights, for other products, does this alter its character: its being a commodity, an exchange value? According to the quantity, it is a commodity of greater or of lesser value, of higher or of lower price.

How then does a sum of commodities, of exchange values, become capital?

Thereby, that as an independent social power, *i.e., as the power of a part of society, it preserves itself and multiplies by exchange with direct, living labour-power.*

The existence of a class which possesses nothing but the ability to work is a necessary presupposition of capital.

It is only the dominion of past, accumulated, materialised labour over immediate living labour that stamps the accumulated labour with the character of capital.

Capital does not consist in the fact that accumulated labour serves living labour as a means for new production. It consists in the fact that living labour serves accumulated labour as the means of preserving and multiplying its exchange value.

CHAPTER VI

RELATION OF WAGE-LABOUR TO CAPITAL

WHAT is it that takes place in the exchange between the capitalist and the wage-labour?

The labourer receives means of subsistence in exchange for his labour-power; but the capitalist receives, in exchange for his means of subsistence, labour, the productive activity of the labourer, the creative force by which the worker not only replaces what he consumes, but also *gives to the accumulated labour a greater value than it previously possessed.* The labourer gets from the capitalist a portion of the existing means of subsistence. For what purpose do these *means of subsistence* serve him? For immediate consumption. But as soon as I consume means of subsistence, they are irrevocably lost to me, unless I employ the time during which these means sustain my life in producing new means of subsistence, in creating by my labour new values in place of the values lost in consumption. But it is just this noble reproductive power that the labourer surrenders to the capitalist in exchange for means of subsistence received. Consequently, he has lost it for himself.

Let us take an example. For one shilling a labourer works all day long in the fields of a farmer, to whom he thus secures a return of two shillings. The farmer not only receives the replaced value which he has given to the day-labourer; he has doubled it. Therefore he has consumed the one shilling that he gave to the day-labourer in a fruitful, productive manner. For the one shilling he has bought the labour-power of the day-labourer, which creates products of the soil of twice the value, and out of one shilling makes two. The day-labourer, on the contrary, receives in the place of his productive force, whose results he has just surrendered to the farmer, one shilling, which he exchanges for *means of subsistence,* which he consumes more or less quickly. The one shilling has therefore been consumed in a double manner—*reproductively* for the capitalist, for it has been exchanged for labour-power, which brought forth two shillings; *unproductively* for the worker, for it has been exchanged for means of subsistence which are lost for ever, and whose value he can obtain again only by repeating the same exchange with the farmer. *Capital therefore presupposes wage-labour; wage-labour presupposes capital. They condition each other; each brings the other into existence.*

Does a worker in a cotton factory produce only cotton goods? No. He produces capital. He produces values which serve anew to command his work and to create by means of it new values.

Capital can multiply itself only by exchanging itself for labour-power, by calling wage-labour into life. The labour-power of the wage-labourer can exchange itself for capital only by increasing capital, by strengthening that very power whose slave it is. *Increase of capital, therefore, is increase of the proletariat, i.e., of the working class.*

And so, the bourgeoisie and its economists maintain that the interest of the capitalist and of the labourer is the same. And in fact, so they are! The worker perishes if capital does not keep him busy. Capital perishes if it does not exploit labour-power, which, in order to exploit, it must buy. The more quickly the capital destined for production—the productive capital—increases, the more prosperous industry is, the more the bourgeoisie enriches itself, the better business gets, so many more workers does the capitalist need, so much the dearer does the worker sell himself. *The fastest possible growth of productive capital is, therefore, the indispensable condition for a tolerable life to the labourer.*

But what is growth of productive capital? Growth of the power of accumulated labour over living labour; growth of the rule of the bourgeoisie over the working class. When wage-labour produces the alien wealth of dominating it, the power hostile to it, capital, there flow back to it its means of employment, *i.e.,* its means of subsistence, under the condition that it again become a part of capital, that it become again the lever whereby capital is to be forced into an accelerated expansive movement.

To say that the interests of capital and the interests of the workers are identical, signifies only this, that capital and wage-labour are two sides of one and the same relation. The one conditions the other in the same way that the usurer and the borrower condition each other.

As long as the wage-labourer remains a wage-labourer, his lot is dependent upon capital. That is what the boasted community of interests between worker and capitalists amounts to.

If capital grows, the mass of wage-labour grows, the number of wage-workers increases; in a word, the sway of capital extends over a greater mass of individuals.

Let us suppose the most favourable case: if productive capital grows, the demand for labour grows. It therefore increases the price of labour-power, wages.

A house may be large or small; as long as the neighbouring houses are likewise small, it satisfies all social requirements for a residence. But let there arise next to the little house a palace, and the little house shrinks into a hut. The little house now makes it clear that its inmate has no social position at all to maintain, or but a very insignificant one; and however high it may shoot up in the course of civilisation, if the neighbouring palace rises in equal or even in greater measure, the occupant of the relatively little house will always find himself more uncomfortable, more dissatisfied, more cramped within his four walls.

An appreciable rise in wages presupposes a rapid growth of productive capital. Rapid growth of productive capital calls forth just as rapid a growth of wealth, of luxury, of social needs and social pleasures. Therefore, although the pleasures of the labourer have increased, the social gratification which they afford has fallen in comparison with the increased pleasures of the capitalist, which are inaccessible to the worker, in comparison with the stage of development of society in general. Our wants and pleasures have their origin in society; we therefore measure them in relation to society; we do not measure them in relation to the objects which serve for their gratification. Since they are of a social nature, they are of a relative nature.

But wages are not at all determined merely by the sum of commodities for which they may be exchanged. Other factors enter into the problem. What the workers directly receive for their labour-power is a certain sum of money. Are wages determined merely by this money price?

In the sixteenth century the gold and silver circulation in Europe increased in consequence of the discovery of richer and more easily worked mines in America. The value of gold and silver, therefore, fell in relation to other commodities. The workers received the same amount of coined silver for their labour-power as before. The money price of their work remained the same, and yet their wages had fallen, for in exchange for the same amount of silver they obtained a smaller amount of other commodities. This was one of the circumstances which furthered the growth of capital, the rise of the bourgeoisie, in the eighteenth century.

Let us take another case. In the winter of 1847, in consequence of bad harvests, the most indispensable means of subsistence—grains, meat, butter, cheese, etc.—rose greatly in price. Let us suppose that the workers still received the same sum of money for their labour-power as before. Did not their wages fall? To be sure. For the same money they received in exchange less bread, meat, etc. Their wages fell, not because the value of silver was less, but because the value of the means of subsistence had increased.

Finally, let us suppose that the money price of labour-power remained the same, while all agricultural and manufactured commodities had fallen in price because of the employment of new machines, of favourable seasons, etc. For the same money the workers could now buy more commodities of all kinds. Their wages have therefore risen, just because their money value has not changed.

The money price of labour-power, the nominal wages, do not therefore coincide with the actual or real wages, *i.e.*, with the amount of commodities which are actually given in exchange for the wages. If then we speak of a rise or fall of wages, we have to keep in mind not only the money price of labour-power, the nominal wages, but also the real wages.

But neither the nominal wages, *i.e.*, the amount of money for which the labourer sells himself to the capitalist, nor the real wages, *i.e.*, the amount of commodities which he can buy for this money, exhausts the relations which are comprehended in the term wages.

Wages are determined above all by their relations to the gain, the profit, of the capitalist. In other words, wages are a proportionate, relative quantity.

Real wages express the price of labour-power in relation to the price of other commodities; *relative wages*, on the other hand, express the share of immediate labour in the value newly created by it, in relation to the share of it which falls to accumulated labour, to capital.

CHAPTER VII

THE GENERAL LAW THAT DETERMINES THE RISE AND FALL OF WAGES AND PROFITS

WE have said: "Wages are not a share of the worker in the commodities produced by him. Wages are that part of already existing commodities with which the capitalist buys a certain amount of productive labour-power." But the capitalist must replace these wages out of the price for which he sells the product made by the worker; he must so replace it that, as a rule, there remains to him a surplus above the cost of production expended by him, that is, he must get a profit.

The selling price of the commodities produced by the worker is divided, from the point of view of the capitalist, into three parts: *First,* the replacement of the price of the raw materials advanced by him, in addition to the replacement of the wear and tear of the tools, machines, and other instruments of labour likewise advanced by him; *second,* the replacement of the wages advanced; and *third,* the surplus left over, *i.e.,* the profit of the capitalist.

While the first part merely replaces *previously existing values,* it is evident that the replacement of the wages and the surplus (the profit of capital) are as a whole taken out of the *new value,* which is *produced by the labour of the worker* and added to the raw materials. And *in this sense* we can view wages as well as profit, for the purpose of comparing them with each other, as shares in the product of the worker.

Real wages may remain the same, they may even rise, nevertheless the relative wages may fall. Let us suppose, for instance, that all means of subsistence have fallen two-thirds in price, while the day's wages have fallen but one-third; for example, from three to two shillings. Although the worker can now get a greater amount of commodities with these two shillings than he formerly did with three shillings, yet his wages have decreased in proportion to the gain of the capitalist. The profit of the capitalist—the manufacturer's for instance—has increased by one shilling, which means that for a smaller amount of exchange values, which he pays to the worker, the latter must produce a greater amount of exchange values than before. The share of capital in proportion to the share of labour has risen. The distribution of social wealth between capital and labour has become still more unequal. The capitalist commands a greater amount of labour with the same capital. The power of the capitalist class over the working class has grown, the social position of the worker has become worse, has been forced down still another degree below that of the capitalist.

What, then, is the general law that determines the rise and fall of wages and profit in their reciprocal relation?

They stand in inverse proportion to each other. The share of (profit) increases in the same proportion in which the share of labour (wages) falls, and vice versa. Profit rises in the same degree in which wages fall; it falls in the same degree in which wages rise.

It might perhaps be argued that the capitalist can gain by an advantageous exchange of his products with other capitalists, by a rise in the demand for his commodities, whether in consequence of the opening up of new markets, or in consequence of temporarily increased demands in the old markets, and so on; that the profit of the capitalist, therefore, may be multiplied by taking advantage of other capitalists, independently of the rise and fall of wages, of the exchange value of labour-power; or that the profit of the capitalist may also rise through improvements in the instruments of labour, new applications of the forces of nature, and so on.

But in the first place it must be admitted that the result remains the same, although brought about in an opposite manner. Profit, indeed, has not risen because wages have fallen, but wages have fallen because profit has risen. With the same amount of another man's labour the capitalist has bought a larger amount of exchange values without having paid more for the labour on that account, *i.e.*, the work is paid for less in proportion to the net gain which it yields to the capitalist.

In the second place, it must be borne in mind that, despite the fluctuations in the prices of commodities, the average price of every commodity, the proportion in which it exchanges for other commodities, is determined by its cost of production. The acts of overreaching and taking advantage of one another within the capitalist ranks necessarily equalise themselves. The improvements of machinery, the new applications of the forces of nature in the service of production, make it possible to produce in a given period of time, with the same amount of labour and capital, a larger amount of products, but in no wise a larger amount of exchange values. If by the use of the spinning-machine I can furnish twice as much yarn in an hour as before its invention—for instance, one hundred pounds instead of fifty pounds—in the long run I receive back, in exchange for this one hundred pounds no more commodities than I did before for fifty; because the cost of production has fallen by one-half, or because I can furnish double the product at the same cost.

Finally, in whatsoever proportion the capitalist class, whether of one country or of the entire world-market, distribute the net revenue of production among themselves, the total amount of this net revenue always consists exclusively of the amount by which accumulated labour has been increased from the proceeds of direct labour. This whole amount, therefore, grows in the same proportion in which labour augments capital, *i.e.,* in the same proportion in which profit rises as compared with wages.

CHAPTER VIII

THE INTERESTS OF CAPITAL AND WAGE-LABOUR ARE DIAMETRICALLY OPPOSED—EFFECT OF GROWTH OF PRODUCTIVE CAPITAL ON WAGES

WE thus see *that, even if we keep ourselves within the relation of capital and wage-labour, the interests of capital and the interests of wage-labour are diametrically opposed to each other.*

A rapid growth of capital is synonymous with a rapid growth of profits. Profits can grow rapidly only when the price of labour—the relative wages—decrease just as rapidly. Relative wages may fall, although real wages rise simultaneously with nominal wages, with the money value of labour, provided only that the real wage does not rise in the same proportion as the profit. If, for instance, in good business years wages rise 5 per cent. while profits rise 30 per cent., the proportional, the relative wage has not *increased,* but *decreased.*

If, therefore, the income of the worker increases with the rapid growth of capital, there is at the same time a widening of the social chasm that divides the worker from the capitalist, an increase in the power of capital over labour, a greater dependence of labour upon capital.

To say that "the worker has an interest in the rapid growth of capital," means only this; that the more speedily the worker augments the wealth of the capitalist, the larger will be the crumbs which fall to him, the greater will be the number of workers that can be called into existence, the more can the mass of slaves dependent upon capital be increased.

We have thus seen that even the *most favourable situation* for the working class, namely, the most rapid growth of capital, however much it may improve the material life of the worker, does not abolish the antagonism between his interests and the interests of the capitalist. *Profit and wages* remain as before, ***in inverse proportion.***

If capital grows rapidly, wages may rise, but the profit of capital rises disproportionately faster. The material position of the worker has improved, but at the cost of his social position. The social chasm that separates him from the capitalist has widened.

Finally, to say that "the most favourable condition for wage-labour is the fastest possible growth of productive capital," is the same as to say: the quicker the working class multiplies and augments the power inimical to it—the wealth of another which lords it over that class—the more favourable will be the conditions under which it will be permitted to toil anew at the multiplication of bourgeois wealth, at the enlargement of the power of capital, content thus to forge for itself the golden chains by which the bourgeoisie drags it in its train.

Growth of productive capital and rise of wages, are they really so indissolubly united as the bourgeois economists maintain? We must not believe their mere words. We dare not believe them even when they claim that the fatter capital is the more will its slave be pampered. The bourgeoisie is too much enlightened, it keeps its accounts much too carefully, to share the prejudices of the feudal lord, who makes an ostentatious display of the magnificence of his retinue. The conditions of existence of the bourgeoisie compel it to attend carefully to its bookkeeping. We must therefore examine more closely into the following question:

In what manner does the growth of productive capital affect wages?

If as a whole, the productive capital of bourgeois society grows, there takes place a more many-sided accumulation of labour. The individual capitals increase in number and in magnitude. The multiplications of individual capitals *increases the competition among capitalists.* The *increasing magnitude* of individual capitals provides the means for *leading more powerful armies of workers with more gigantic instruments of war upon the industrial battlefield.*

The one capitalist can drive the other from the field and carry off his capital only by selling more cheaply. In order to sell more cheaply without ruining himself, he must produce more cheaply, *i.e.,* increase the productive force of labour as much as possible.

But the productive power of labour is increased above all by a *greater division of labour* and by a more general introduction and constant improvement of *machinery*. The larger the army of workers among whom the labour is subdivided, the more gigantic the scale upon which machinery is introduced, the more in proportion does the cost of production decrease, the more fruitful is the labour. And so there arises among the capitalists a universal rivalry for the increase of the division of labour and of machinery and for their exploitation upon the greatest possible scale.

If, now, by a greater division of labour, by the application and improvement of new machines, by a more advantageous exploitation of the forces of nature on a larger scale, a capitalist has found the means of producing with the same amount of labour (whether it be direct or accumulated labour) a larger amount of products of commodities than his competitors—if, for instance, he can produce a whole yard of linen in the same labour-time in which his competitors weave half a yard—how will this capitalist act?

He could keep on selling half a yard of linen at the old market price; but this would not have the effect of driving his opponents from the field and enlarging his own market. But his need of a market has increased in the same measure in which his productive power has extended. The more powerful and costly means of production that he has called into existence *enable* him, it is true, to sell his wares more cheaply, but they *compel* him at the same time *to sell more wares,* to get control of a very much *greater* market for his commodities; consequently, this capitalist will sell his half yard of linen more cheaply than his competitors.

But the capitalist will not sell the whole yard so cheaply as his competitors sell the half yard, although the production of the whole yard costs no more to him than does that of the half yard to the others. Otherwise he would make no extra profit, and would get back in exchange only the cost of production. He might obtain a greater income from having set in motion a larger capital, but not from having made a greater profit on his capital than the others. Moreover, he attains the object he is aiming at if he prices his goods only a small percentage lower than his competitors. He drives them off the field, he wrests from them at least a part of their market, by *underselling* them.

And finally, let us remember that the current price always stands either *above or below the cost of production,* according as the sale of a commodity takes place in the favourable or unfavourable period of the industry. According as the market price of the yard of linen stands above or below its former cost of production, will the percentage vary at which the capitalist who has made use of the new and more fruitful means of production sell above his real cost of production.

But the *privilege* of our capitalist is not of long duration. Other competing capitalists introduce the same machines, the same division of labour, and introduce them upon the same or even upon a greater scale. And finally this introduction becomes so universal that the price of the linen is lowered not only below its old, but even below its new cost of production.

The capitalists therefore find themselves, in their mutual relations, in the same situation in which they were before the introduction of the new means of production; and if they are by these means enabled to offer double the product at the old price, they are now forced to furnish double the product for less than the old price. Having arrived at the new point, the new cost of production, the battle for supremacy in the market has to be fought out anew. Given more division of labour and more machinery, and there results a greater scale upon which division of labour and machinery are exploited. And competition again brings the same reaction against this result.

CHAPTER IX

EFFECT OF CAPITALIST COMPETITION ON THE CAPITALIST CLASS, THE MIDDLE CLASS, AND THE WORKING CLASS

We thus see how the method of production and the means of production are constantly enlarged, revolutionised, how *division of labour necessarily draws after it greater division of labour, the employment of machinery greater employment of machinery, work upon a large scale work upon a still greater scale.* This is the law that continually throws capitalist production out of its old ruts and compels capital to strain ever more the productive forces of labour *for the very reason* that it has already strained them—the law that grants it no respite, and constantly shouts in its ear: March! march! This is no other law than that which, within the periodical fluctuations of commerce, necessarily *adjusts the price of a commodity to its cost of production.*

No matter how powerful the means of production which a capitalist may bring into the field, competition will make their adoption general; and from the moment that they have been generally adopted, the sole result of the greater productiveness of his capital will be that he must furnish *at the same price,* ten, twenty, one hundred times as much as before. But since he must find a market for, perhaps, a thousand times as much, in order to outweigh the lower selling price by the greater quantity of the sales; since now a more extensive sale is necessary not only to gain a greater profit, but also in order to replace the cost of production (the instrument of production itself grows always more costly, as we have seen), and since this more extensive sale has become a question of life and death not only for him, but also for his rivals, the old struggle must begin again, and it is all the more violent the more powerful the means of production already invented are. *The division of labour and the application of machinery will therefore take a fresh start, and upon an even greater scale.*

Whatever be the power of the means of production which are

employed, competition seeks to rob capital of the golden fruits of this power by reducing the price of commodities to the cost of production; in the same measure in which production is cheapened, *i.e.,* in the same measure in which more can be produced with the same amount of labour, it compels by a law which is irresistible a still greater cheapening of production, the sale of ever greater masses of product for smaller prices. Thus the capitalist will have gained nothing more by his efforts than the obligation to furnish a greater product in the same labour-time; in a word, more difficult conditions for the profitable employment of his capital. While competition, therefore, constantly pursues him with its law of the cost of production and turns against himself every weapon that he forges against his rivals, the capitalist continually seeks to get the best of competition by restlessly introducing further subdivision of labour and new machines, which, though more expensive, enable him to produce more cheaply, instead of waiting until the new machines shall have been rendered obsolete by competition.

If we now conceive this feverish agitation as it operates in the *market of the whole world,* we shall be in a position to comprehend how the growth, accumulation, and concentration of capital bring in their train an ever more detailed subdivision of labour, an ever greater improvement of old machines, and a constant application of new machines—a process which goes on uninterruptedly, with feverish haste, and upon an ever more gigantic scale.

But what effect do these conditions, which are inseparable from the growth of productive capital, have upon the determination of wages?

The greater *division of labour* enables one labourer to accomplish the work of five, ten, or twenty labourers; it therefore increases competition among the labourers fivefold, tenfold, or twentyfold. The labourers compete not only by selling themselves one cheaper than the other, but also by one doing the work of five, then ten, or twenty; and they are forced to compete in this manner by the division of labour, which is introduced and steadily improved by capital.

Furthermore, to the same degree in which the division of labour increases, is the labour simplified. The special skill of the labourer becomes worthless. He becomes transformed into a simple monotonous force of production, with neither physical nor mental elasticity. His work becomes accessible to all; therefore competitors press upon him from all sides. Moreover, it must be remembered that the more simple, the more easily learned the work is, so much the less is its cost of production, the expense of its acquisition, and so much the lower must the wages sink—for, like the price of any other commodity, they are determined by the cost of production. Therefore, *in the same measure in which labour becomes more unsatisfactory, more repulsive, do competition increase and wages decrease.*

The labourer seeks to maintain the total of his wages for a given time by performing more labour, either by working a greater number of hours, or by accomplishing more in the same number of hours. Thus, urged on by want, he himself multiplies the disastrous effects of division of labour. The result is: *the more he works, the less wages he receives.* And for this simple reason: the more he works, the more he competes against his fellow workmen, the more he compels them to compete against him, and to offer themselves on the same wretched conditions as he does; so that, in the last analysis, *he competes against himself as a member of the working class.*

Machinery produces the same effects, but upon a much larger scale. It supplants skilled labourers by unskilled, men by women, adults by children; where newly introduced, it throws workers upon the streets in great masses; and as it becomes more highly developed and more productive it discards them in additional though smaller numbers.

We have hastily sketched in broad outlines the *industrial war of capitalists among themselves. This war has the peculiarity that the battles in it are won less by recruiting than by discharging the army of workers. The generals (the capitalists) vie with one another as to who can discharge the greatest number of industrial soldiers.*

The economists tell us, to be sure, that those labourers who have been rendered superfluous by machinery find new avenues of employment. They dare not assert directly that the same labourers that have been discharged find situations in new branches of labour. Facts cry out too loudly against this lie. Strictly speaking, they only maintain that new means of employment will be found *for other sections of the working class;* for example, for that portion of the young generation of labourers who were about to enter upon that branch of industry which had just been abolished. Of course, this is a great satisfaction to the disabled labourers. There will be no lack of fresh exploitable blood and muscle for the Messrs. Capitalists—the dead may bury their dead. This consolation seems to be intended more for the comfort of the capitalists themselves than of their labourers. If the whole class of the wage-labourer were to be annihilated by machinery, how terrible that would be for capital, *which, without wage-labour, ceases to be capital!*

But even if we assume that all who are directly forced out of employment by machinery, as well as all of the rising generation who were waiting for a chance of employment in the same branch of industry, do actually find some new employment—are we to believe that this new employment will pay as high wages as did the one they have lost? If it did, *it would be in contradiction to all the laws of political economy.* We have seen how modern industry always tends to the substitution of the simpler and more subordinate employments for the higher and more complex ones. How, then, could a mass of workers thrown out of one branch of industry by machinery find refuge in another branch, unless they were to be paid more poorly?

An exception to the law has been adduced, namely, the workers who are employed in the manufacture of machinery itself. As soon as there is in industry a greater demand for and a greater consumption of machinery, it is said that the number of machines must necessarily increase; consequently, also, the manufacture of machines; consequently, also, the employment of workers in machine manufacture;—and the workers employed in this branch of industry are skilled, even educated, workers.

Since the year 1840 this assertion, which even before that date was only half true, has lost all semblance of truth; for the most diverse machines are now applied to the manufacture of the machines themselves on quite as extensive a scale as in the manufacture of cotton yarn, and the labourers employed in machine factories can but play the rôle of very stupid machines alongside of the highly ingenious machines.

But in place of the man who has been dismissed by the machine, the factory may employ, perhaps, three children and one woman! And must not the wages of the man have previously sufficed for the three children and one woman? Must not the minimum wages have sufficed for the preservation and propagation of the race? What, then, do these beloved bourgeois phrases prove? Nothing more than that now four times as many workers' lives are used up as there were previously, in order to obtain the livelihood of one working family.

To sum up: *the more productive capital grows, the more it extends the division of labour and the application of machinery; the more the division of labour and the application of machinery extend, the more does competition extend among the workers, the more do their wages shrink together.*

In addition, the working class is also recruited from the *higher strata* of society; a mass of small business men and of people living upon the interest of their capitals is precipitated into the ranks of the working class, and they will have nothing else to do than to stretch out their arms alongside of the arms of the workers. Thus the forest of outstretched arms, begging for work, grows ever thicker, while the arms themselves grow ever leaner.

It is evident that the small manufacturer cannot survive in a struggle in which the first condition of success is production upon an ever greater scale. It is evident that the small manufacturer cannot at the same time be a big manufacturer.

That the interest on capital decreases in the same ratio in which the mass and number of capitals increase, that it diminishes with the growth of capital, that therefore the small capitalist can no longer live on his interest, but must consequently throw himself upon industry by joining the ranks of the small manufacturers and thereby increasing the number of candidates for the proletariat—all this requires no further elucidation.

Finally, in the same measure in which the capitalists are compelled, by the movement described above, to exploit the already existing gigantic means of production on an ever-increasing scale, and for this purpose to set in motion all the mainsprings of credit, in the same measure do they increase the industrial earthquakes, in the midst of which the commercial world can preserve itself only by sacrificing a portion of its wealth, its products, and even its forces of production, to the gods of the lower world—in short, the *crises* increase. They become more frequent and more violent, if for no other reason, than for this alone, that in the same measure in which the mass of products grows, and therefore the needs for extensive markets, in the same measure does the world market shrink ever more, and ever fewer markets remain to be exploited, since every previous crisis has subjected to the commerce of the world a hitherto unconquered or but superficially exploited market.

But capital not only lives upon labour. Like a master, at once distinguished and barbarous, it drags with it into its grave the corpses of its slaves, whole hecatombs of workers, who perish in the crises.

We thus see that *if capital grows rapidly, competition among the workers grows with even greater rapidity, i.e., the means of employment and subsistence for the working class decrease in proportion even more rapidly; but, this notwithstanding, the rapid growth of capital is the most favourable condition for wage-labour.*